To

Love

Jean

+ Mum

WHEN NIGHTS WERE LONG

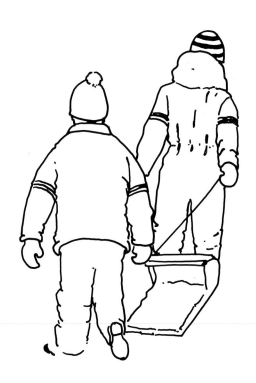

P. Shostak
Nov. '82

WHEN NIGHTS WERE LONG

Paintings and text by Peter Shostak

Yalenka Books of Victoria, B.C.

Printed in Canada

First printing

I.S.B.N. 0-9691180-0-7

When Nights Were Long
is published by

Yalenka Enterprises Inc.
P.O. Box 4191, Stn. A
Victoria, B.C.
V8X 3X7
Phone: (604) 658-8785

This book is dedicated to my family, who were part of the work and play activities of my childhood; to all children, for whom nights come too soon; as well as, to all parents, who through the stimulation of the images and writing will take time to share their own experiences, when nights were long.

WHEN NIGHTS WERE LONG

It's already dark outside.

The first eighteen years of my life were spent on a farm in Northeastern Alberta. My experiences, I am sure, were parallel to those of many, who grew up under similar circumstances.

Late fall and winter months of long nights are the basis for this series of paintings.

The phenomenon, of days getting shorter, went relatively unnoticed during late summer and early fall. It was not until October that we quickly ran out of daylight.

After arriving from school, we had something to eat and then started in on whatever had to be done. On a farm, there never was a shortage of tasks and daily chores. With luck, on some days, our regular chores were the only responsibilities for the evening, enabling us to use any extra time for whatever we wanted to do. Chores came first and because the daylight period gradually diminished, there came a time when there just was no daylight remaining for our own activities. During school days, life on a farm, for almost four months, meant doing everything, including chores, in the dark. On weekends, it was a treat to be able to see your own farm in the daylight hours.

We quickly learned what had to be completed first, before it got too dark. Indoor tasks, such as feeding and watering the chickens and pigs, were usually done first, as it became so dark inside the buildings. In the main barn, a lantern was used, but it was lit only when Dad was also in the barn, as risk of fire was always so great. Outside activities, such as feeding cows and bringing water and wood to the house, were done last. The snow, covering everything, made whatever light remained last a bit longer. After we got electricity on the farm, things changed, as several outdoor lights helped push back the darkness.

Along with the increasing darkness came the cold. On many nights one did not venture outside after chores were finished.

Maybe after we finish our chores . . .

Our farm was a mixed farm; that is, one where we had a little of everything. Especially during winter, all of the animals depended on us for their daily food, water and shelter. Whenever animals were involved, there were no holidays from daily chores. Morning and evening, one had to attend to a number of duties.

During the weekdays, chores were basically the same from day to day, unless some unexpected event took place, which would disrupt the regular pattern of activities. If a cow gave birth to a calf, by the strawpile, it was then necessary to haul the calf home in the small sleigh used for hauling wood to the house. Unexpected events, such as this, were greeted as a welcome change from the daily routine.

Our family was fortunate, in a way, as there were five boys. This meant we could divide the various jobs among ourselves. One-child farm families had definitely a more difficult life. The easiest tasks, such as bringing wood to the house, feeding the cats, and collecting the eggs, were delegated to the younger members, while the more difficult ones, of feeding the pigs and tending to the cattle, were the responsibilities of the older boys.

Since daily chores were a fact of life on every farm, Sunday games of hockey always had to be terminated when it was time to go home and tend to the waiting animals. If the weather was not too cold and it was quite bright outside, due to moon and star light, we resumed our games after the chores were finished and we had had something to eat. But, more often than not, the tired bodies, after a hot meal, just did not want to venture out of the warm house.

Bringing water to the chicken coop.

The long, harsh winters were so hard on the farm animals. In order that they would survive, most of these animals were sheltered in their respective buildings. When the weather turned exceptionally cold, even all of the cattle were somehow fitted into the barn. Horses, which were the hardiest animals, relied solely on the protection of the outdoor shed or straw-pile, while the farm dogs, friends of few, if any, of the other farm animals, had their own nest, usually in the haypile by the barn.

Most of the farm buildings were quite small and not all that solid. Somehow, the combination of the insulating layers of snow outside and the body heat of the animals inside was adequate to keep them relatively warm, even through the coldest periods. When tending to the animals we made sure that the door was not kept open for any length of time.

Regardless of how big or small the animals were, they all depended on us for their daily food and water. Carrying water, to the various sheds housing the animals, was a task performed at least twice daily. A small wood heater, in the main water tank, next to the well, was used to warm the water, making it easier for the animals to drink. Making a fire in this heater was the first task of each winter morning.

Although there was a division of labour and everyone was responsible for certain duties, Dad was the one to do a quick check to make sure everything was done. He was always last to come into the house for the night. On occasion, if one of us forgot to do a task, he would ask about it. To learn a lesson, the forgetful person had to get dressed and leave the warmth of the house to go and complete it. If it was really cold outside, Dad took pity on us and did the chore himself before coming in.

By tending daily to the various animals, we were very familiar with them. All of the cows and horses had names, and certainly, distinct personalities. Some were very gentle and easy to handle, while others took advantage of your small size and made life miserable. One of our black cows just did not allow any of the boys to tie her up in the barn. Any attempts were met with a quick head butt to the stomach, sending an individual for a ride on the floor. As we grew older and braver, we learned to challenge her and eventually won the battle. Usually any approach, which was confident, stern and showed no fear, caused the animal to back off and behave.

Even though our world was relatively simple and we learned about cities and far away places through books, we did not feel that we were missing anything.

99,100, here I come.

In late fall, after the harvest was in, and before the weather got too cold, we took advantage of the evening light by playing some of our favourite games.

One of these games was Hide and Seek, later referred to as Kick the Can. On our farm, we preferred to play this game at dusk when the lack of light made hiding easier, and more adventurous, but also, dangerous.

Occasionally, injuries would result from running into or tripping over objects while running to home base. One such accident left a permanent scar on my face, after I ran into a barbed wire which had been strung across the cattle gate. One method of keeping the larger cattle out of the barnyard, while still permitting access for the calves, was to string a wire across the open gate at a height of about four feet. The wire was in place when I ran into it at full force.

The more participants in the game, the more interesting and exciting it became. We especially enjoyed playing when a neighbouring family, with their children, came to visit. Playing in your own yard provided a definite advantage, as you knew every part of your yard and where the good hiding places were. Sometimes the odds were evened out when the family dog became involved, following you to your hiding place, and in turn, giving you away. Regardless of how hard I tried, I never found a way to make a good Hide and Seek player of our dog.

The age of the participants determined if there would be special considerations and if rules of the game would be modified. One rule modification permitted young players to count only to twenty or so. Otherwise, waiting for a five or six year old to count to one hundred meant that you, cramped in your hiding place, waited a long time. Pretending not to see the young players in their hiding places, or giving them a good head start in running to home base were other ways of making them feel as important a part of the game as any of the older members.

Hallowe'en Pranks.

One evening which did not come soon enough was that of October 31. Hallowe'en was a night of tricks and not treats; a night to carry out deeds planned well in advance; a night to provide material for many winter evenings of stories and laughter.

As young children, we looked forward to this day, not only because of the grand school party complete with masks, costumes, candies and apples, but, also, in anticipation of what tricks would be done to our farm. Since the tricksters were all good-humoured, it was almost like a game between them and the farmers. Waking up in the morning, to find that your farm had been untouched, was a real letdown.

The pranks were performed by the older boys in the dead of night, well after everyone had gone to bed. A planning session of where to go and what to do was held in advance of this day, as it was necessary to be equipped with appropriate tools. The older and more experienced the group the more daring they became and it was a challenge to visit farms where they probably would have someone waiting for them with a shotgun loaded with salt. Farms where there were one or two noisy dogs were hard to visit undetected but each year the light of the next morning would let everyone know what had been done during the dark hours.

Harnessing cows in horse harnesses, placing bells on pigs, carrying sleeping turkeys from their roost and placing them in the outhouse or other unlikely locations were all deeds sure to provide hours of laughter in the months to come.

Positioning a box or heavy sack over the farmhouse chimney was a daring trick which, if successfully completed, would be the first noticed in the morning when someone would attempt to light a fire in the stove. Next to our two-room school were two teacherages. Covering the chimney was a common trick, especially if the teacher was a young lady. Next morning she would have to wait patiently in the cold until someone would be kind enough to climb up and remove the covering.

In certain instances, after tricks were completed and the farmer had not awakened, the final act was to deliberately make enough noise to wake everyone up and see how the intruders would be treated. It was not fun if the reaction was very mild. Farmers, in their bare feet, pants held up with one hand and a shotgun in the other, madly shouting and cursing the unseen pranksters, or better still, chasing one of them, was the stuff good stories were made of.

Where do all the pretty brides go?

As children, we did not fully grasp how long a night was until we had an opportunity to stay up as late as our bodies would permit. This occurred when, along with the entire family, we attended a wedding held on one of the neighbouring farms. It was the practice to have the children accompany their parents to such social events. Being able to go to a wedding was not only a treat but a great learning experience. These celebrations were at least a one day and night affair but for us one night was long enough.

To house the wedding party and guests, either a temporary structure was erected near the farmhouse, or a dance floor was built and then covered with a rented tent. Two empty granaries were dragged to the site; one to serve as an extension of the kitchen; the other, as a source of liquid refreshments. For several days before the wedding, friends and neighbours assisted with preparation of both facilities and large quantities of food.

We looked forward to this event with much excitement. Musicians were an important part of all wedding parties. While running around, we periodically stopped to watch them set up and tune their instruments, and maybe sneak in several thumps on the drum with the foot pedal.

As the parents became involved in the celebrations, older children were left to fend for themselves. One of the hardworking ladies in the kitchen always saw that we did not go hungry and sometimes, the men, carrying pitchers of foamy draft beer, would partly fill our empty glasses.

Weddings were very emotional events. We were not quite sure why crying was necessary but at intervals the laughter, singing and dancing would be dampened by tears.

Weddings were also a time for exploration. On one occasion, we went into a bedroom of the farmhouse, where we found some bright red nail polish. This one and only experience with polish proved it was easy to put on but almost impossible to take off. What a way to put a damper on a still young night as we walked around with our hands in our pockets interspersed with futile attempts at scratching the polish off. One nail would have been plenty but ten were too many.

Weddings provided opportunities to make new friends; to realize that not all of the young ladies and men were on the dance floor; to find out that cigarettes were not that great; and, to learn that there was a reason why the foamy beer was given to us in such small quantities.

As the hours went by, our running around and making a nuisance of ourselves slowed down, and, one by one, newfound friends disappeared and eventually, we also looked for a place to fall asleep. Although it seemed that parents did not know what you were up to, they always appeared in time to direct you to the room in the farmhouse where you would find the other children already asleep. Much later, still in darkness, you would vaguely remember being awakened to go home. The nights were sure long.

This will probably be my best angel.

Whereas the first major snowfall of late October or November meant that we would have to live with this white covering for almost six months, our jubilation over its arrival was not diminished. Our drab, almost colourless environment was instantly transformed into a world of white. Even if we so looked forward to the day when it would snow, we never were fully prepared for the consequences. A variety of tools and play items were left outside only to be covered up. Some of these articles remained hidden until the warm spring sun melted the snow and revealed their place of hibernation.

The snow-covered yard and fields resembled enormous pieces of white paper which were soon marked by the trails and footprints of people and animals moving across the surface. We delighted in making our marks in this white, fluffy powder by walking, running and rolling around. Games of Follow the Leader and Fox and Geese were played. Patterns were made and angels appeared wherever there remained undisturbed areas of snow.

Any movement and activity was imprinted for all to see. On one sad occasion, my footprints, leading to the rail fence by the barn, revealed to my father that I had discovered what had happened to one of our cats.

Through the first grade readers, my farm world was expanded to include the city life of Dick, Jane, Sally, Tim and Puff. It was from one of these readers that I got the idea of making a leash for my cat. Cut twine, which previously had bound sheaves of oats, was used. After wrestling with the farm cat, who had no desire to become a fancy city cat, I finally tied the twine around his neck. Try as I would, he just did not want to play this game with me and at the first opportunity escaped with the twine trailing behind him. I last saw him running towards the barn and wondered what happened to him as he did not appear again at the house.

Cats do not like water, nor do they like to walk in fresh, unpacked snow. After running away, this unfortunate cat ran along the top rail of the fence surrounding the piles of hay and when he came to the corner post he jumped off and caught the trailing twine between the post and the rail. Several days later, when I went to the haypile, I saw how this cat lost all nine lives. I was greatly disturbed by the fact that my actions led to the death of a favourite pet.

It is Leonard's turn to be the fox.

A fresh snowfall, covering previous tracks and trails, again provided large white areas, where new lines and patterns were created.

A game which required an area of undisturbed snow was that of Fox and Geese. It began, like a ritual, with all of the participants following a leader, who proceeded to tramp a large circle through the snow. Not everyone had the ability to lead the group in forming this critical outside rim. I do not know why, but it was very important to start with a perfect circle.

The farm dog, who liked to participate, learned to follow the group rather than set out on his own through the snow. If the snow was quite deep, then it was necessary to retrace the trails several times in order to pack the snow down. Once this was done, then the dividing lines were made and the game began. The lines radiating from the centre of the circle resembled spokes on a wheel and served as the safety paths for the geese, who were pursued by a fox. Sometimes a small or slow fox had great difficulty in catching one of the geese who taunted and deliberately baited him.

Running in snow was very tiring, so that, before long the game was terminated and something less strenuous was played. Follow the Leader was popular, especially, if the winter winds had packed snow into hard drifts along the fences. We then wound our way along these drifts, as long as the snow held up our weight.

On occasion, as we walked along the fences, we were startled by grouse flying out from their night resting places under the snow. Snow acted as an excellent insulator from the cold air. We often wondered how the few wild birds and animals, which did not migrate or hibernate, managed to survive the long winters. Nature provided the grouse, or partridge, as we called them, with the ability to fly into soft mounds of snow. Like a ball landing, these birds buried themselves and remained there until disturbed. As we became more observant, we perceived markings and telltale signs where grouse had flown into the soft snow.

Exhausted, but with rosy cheeks, we finally came into the house. After an outing, such as this, there was always a pile of woollen mitts and pants, caked with snow, to look after. These items found their place around the woodstove where they first thawed out and were, hopefully, dry by morning for use again. Supplying each of us with at least two pairs of mitts, as well as several pairs of woollen socks, kept my mother and grandmother busy knitting during many long winter evenings.

Don't get your leg caught in the snow.

Two miles from home, the river banks provided us with the largest hills for sledding, as the rest of the landscape was quite flat. Our farm had a few gentle rises, but, the height of these was more imagined than real, and was not very suitable for much more than short rides. We envied anyone who lived on a farm situated near a steep hill.

Whenever we did go to a hill, worthy of sliding down, it was a major expedition. We brought food with us, as well as, an axe, a supply of paper, matches and kindling. On a cold night, the warmth of the fire helped push the stark emptiness of the landscape away and gave us the feeling of having some control over our environment. By taking turns, one of us was kept constantly busy tending the fire and hunting for dry branches and small trees to burn.

The repeated climbing of the hill consumed a great deal of energy, and before long, everyone was ready to eat the food we brought. This food was not fancy, maybe just a few slices of bread and an apple each, but it always tasted so good. Since the bread was frozen solid, we would first thaw it out, and then toast it over the fire. Apples were also cooked, at least the outside was cooked, while the inside remained firm.

Being towed, on skis or a tobaggan, behind a horse-drawn sleigh, was an activity we engaged in frequently. Since the skis were homemade, it gave us a great deal of satisfaction to actually use something which we had made ourselves. Curling up the tips of the two boards, selected to serve as the skis, was the most difficult task. After carefully picking two straight, smooth boards, the tips were cut to form a rounded shape. These tips were then soaked for days in the water tank. The water-softened wood was bent to provide the desired curve. Bending the wood was not such a problem; keeping it bent was, as the tips often flattened out after a day or two.

Leather straps, to accommodate our heavy felt boots, were nailed on to the skis. The skis were waxed and we were ready to try them out. If the homemade equipment did not keep falling apart, we quickly became quite skilled at being towed behind the sleigh.

Later, when there were more and better-maintained roads, and one of the older neighbouring boys had access to a truck or car, we were towed behind a vehicle at much greater speeds. Your ride was over, when you fell down, or, you had travelled a mile along the road over snowbanks, driveways, and other obstacles. It was a wonder that no one was badly hurt during these rides, as the driver of the vehicle, egged on by the passengers, became exuberant and drove at excessive speeds.

Snowbank King at full moon.

A prairie blizzard, lasting two days, made one wonder how any life could withstand and survive in such an environment. The farmer and his family provided food and shelter for their animals, but, beyond the farmyard, it seemed that no life could possibly exist.

When the winds finally subsided and the snow no longer was whipped around in blinding sheets, life began to once more appear on the white landscape. Prairie animals and birds all had their own built-in survival systems. Even the domesticated animals, such as horses, were able to function and survive during the most severe winter storms.

Many farmers owe their lives to the special sense of direction of their horses, who, when given free rein during a blinding blizzard, would manage to find their way back to the farm.

After being cooped up in the house for two days, hard-packed snowbanks were our reward. These fresh snowbanks were initially great for walking and sliding on and, later, for tunneling into. Snowbanks, around the woodpile and water tank, and in doorways, as well as, paths, leading to the various buildings, had to be tackled with a shovel.

These trails of hard-packed snow provided a certain amount of freedom and served as a highway over the frozen world. At what other time could you walk with ease over a five foot fence?

Being first seems to be an inborn characteristic trait of man as well as animals. On the farm, we enjoyed watching some of the animals, especially cattle, playing their version of King of the Castle.

I grew up in an area of Canada where the landscape was relatively flat. Our castles were limited to piles of hay, straw, or snow. Whatever the choice, it was important that the surface one fell on was relatively soft. As a King, you did not reign very long.

Flushed red cheeks were part of being outside in the cold. Sometimes white areas appeared on one's nose, cheeks or ear lobes. This signalled that the cold was winning over the body's heating system and before coming indoors you had to rub some snow over the affected areas. Frost-bite was the price we occasionally paid for the privilege of being outdoors.

What is the score?

My introduction to hockey was in November of my first year of school. The two-room school, which I attended, accommodated all students from grades one to nine and was the source of most information about the world existing beyond the boundaries of our farm community.

After the arrival of winter, the area, where just a month or so earlier we had played softball, was transformed into a hockey rink by the older boys. First, the snow was packed down to form a base; then, blocks of wood were placed in a line around the edge of the proposed ice area. For days, during recess, noon hour, and, before and after school, pail after pail of water was poured on to the slowly forming ice surface. Care was taken not to run the school well dry as this was our only water supply.

As a child who had never seen hockey played, the enthusiasm of the boys in creating an ice surface added to my interest in the game. After days of hard work, the boys agreed that they could begin to play hockey and the following day all arrived at school prepared for the game. Very few students had skates, but all had a stick. The more fortunate had a store-bought one, others had made their own, while several raided the nearby willow bushes in search of a properly curved willow.

Since the game was boisterous, with much shouting, bumping of bodies and loud arguments, the younger children watched from a distance. It was not until a year later that I, too, went to the willow patch in search of my first hockey stick. Subsequently, I made my own at home, using a discarded hockey stick handle and a board for a blade. The life of the home-made stick was usually shorter than the time it took to make it. In appearance they looked satisfactory but the technical problem of attaching the blade to the handle was never adequately solved.

Of course, everyone wanted skates, but this was a luxury not many could afford. Instead, I concentrated on saving my money to buy a real hockey stick and some black tape. The one cent per bottle refund was our main income and it took several months of collecting before we made a trip to town with Dad to make the major one dollar and twenty-five cent purchase.

Shin pads were rolls of newspapers kept in place by rubber jar rings. The heavy winter pants over these pads, all jambed into the standard foot gear of felt boots, provided ample protection against any wildly swung stick or airborne puck.

We spent many evenings playing hockey on a small patch of ice we had made in the farmyard or on a cleared portion of one of the nearby ponds.

Maybe I will get new skates for my birthday.

I attended the country school until October of the sixth grade when it was decided that the school would be closed and everyone would be bussed to a central school some fifteen miles away. From this day on, school took on another meaning as not only did we have to spend hours everyday bouncing around on the hard seats of the bus, but we became part of a large student population where, in my case, I was an insignificant sixth grader in a class of forty-two.

There were many advantages and disadvantages in attending this school. Fortunately, I was able to quickly establish my place in this mass of fellow students and I did find it a challenge to be confronted with an entirely new system of education. For the first time, we became aware and were part of serious schoolground rivalries and confrontations. Divisions existed because of age and grade levels, where you lived, and, most importantly, your ethnic background.

Coming from a small school, where almost everyone was of Ukrainian descent, and suddenly finding yourself in the minority, resulted in having to make many adjustments. Unwritten rules of the playground did not permit easy, free association with newfound classmates. Instead, you had to be on the Ukrainian team which was doing daily battle with the French team.

Since the school had a fairly respectable hockey rink, the pressure on my parents to buy me a pair of skates increased daily. Finally the day arrived when I was told that on Monday, market day, when farmers brought any pigs or cattle they wished to sell to the stockyard in town, Dad would see if he could buy a pair of skates for me. After watching the other students with envy, as they moved so quickly and gracefully on their skates, I could not wait to acquire my own, when I, too, would be able to take part in the hockey games.

Monday finally arrived and Dad came home from town with a pair of skates; not a new pair, but a pair of skates with new tape over the toe section. Tuesday was a long day at school and the bus ride was even longer as I could hardly wait to get home and try out my skates on the small patch of ice we had cleared.

With two pairs of socks, the skates felt snug but as I tried to stand up they bent outward. The big surprise came when I realized that learning to skate was going to be very frustrating and painful and would not happen in one day. I was convinced that there was something drastically wrong with these used, secondhand skates. Anything I attempted to do had no resemblance to the easy, freewheeling style displayed by the students on the hockey rink at school. Playing hockey on skates was not possible, at least not for the first few sessions, as the stick was now needed to keep me from falling down.

Maybe someday we will get to play on a real hockey rink.

Before long, my brothers also had skates and, weather permitting, we spent a great deal of time either on the small patch of ice we created on an unused level portion of the barnyard or on the cleared ice of a nearby pond. A skating area on a pond was usually preferred, as it was much larger than the surface we could flood with water from the well.

Quality of the ice on these ponds varied from year to year with the two prime factors being amount of water in the pond before freeze-up and wind conditions when the first ice formed in late fall. If the summer was very hot with little rain, then the water level would drop and there just would not be enough water area for a decent rink. If it was too windy as the water was freezing, the resulting ice surface would be too rough to skate on.

Regardless of where we played, the task of clearing the snow off the ice seemed to be a never ending one. Some winters, if there was a great deal of snow, our skating area became smaller with each snowstorm. What started out as a fairly large surface was reduced in size as it became too difficult to clear.

How we envied the town kids with their covered rink, free from any snow clearing, and most importantly, its huge, smooth surface complete with blue lines and all. We could only imagine what it would be like to play hockey there.

Sometimes we also had large surfaces to skate on. These were available during late fall after the ice had formed to a depth strong enough to support our weight but before the snow came. You became accustomed to the sound of ice cracking and if you did not hit a muskrat run, where the ice would be thinner than normal, you could skate for miles weaving in and out of the clumps of grass and bulrushes.

In the springtime, after the melting snow had created large ponds, a return to cold weather for several days produced acres of glassy ice. The only problem of playing hockey here was the lack of any boundaries. A hard-shot puck would glide a great distance before it stopped on its own. I still wonder what it would be like to play on a real hockey rink.

Do the cows mind if we play hide and seek here?

The success of a harvest was judged by the size and number of strawpiles. The threshing machine, accompanied by all the noise and dust, separated the grain from the wagonloads of sheaves, and, in the process, chopped up the straw and deposited it into large mounds. The wheat, oats and barley were all stored in separate granaries, which were lined up on the west or southwest side of the piles.

During the long winter, these piles of straw provided the cattle and horses with the bulk of their winter food and served as a refuge and shelter against the bitter cold and wind. Weekly, a load of straw was hauled to the farmyard to provide bedding, in the barns, for the other animals.

Since the cattle preferred the straw of one grain over another, they would, almost like miners, follow the seams, by eating a tunnel into the pile. These tunnels provided additional shelter but were a hazard, as they could either cave in or the weight of the straw and snow would cause a portion of the pile to slide down or topple over.

Dad kept watch over the condition of the strawpile, and, when it appeared that a dangerous situation was at hand, he made certain that all of the cattle were accounted for morning and evening. Since the warm water supply was from the water tank in the barnyard, the cows made a twice daily trek from the strawpile, enabling Dad to easily see if any were missing. If one or two of the animals failed to appear, there was reason for concern.

Armed with a pitchfork, he would walk along the hard-packed path to the pile, prepared for a rescue of the trapped cattle. If the cave-in was not very serious, the rescue did not take very long, but, on occasion, a large amount of straw had to be moved before the buried cattle were freed.

As we became more helpful with the various chores, our assistance was also called upon to help locate and free the animals. This search was always a race against time. With the end of the fork handle, we poked into any holes to see if we could locate the animals. With luck, the victims were soon pin-pointed and freed without any casualities.

On a happier note, the strawpile, with the resting animals, provided another playground. Here, we took part in a variety of games, with Hide and Seek being one of our favourites. Our running around and our attempts at covering ourselves with straw kept the cold away. After a while the enthusiasm of the game wore off and it was time to go home and leave the animals to rest again, undisturbed, in the silence of the winter night.

Two more slides and that's it.

Haystacks always provided a challenge, as they were our mountains to be conquered, even if we had to use a ladder. Once up there, coming down was a different story. It was a matter of time before one of the group was talked into sliding down and landing on the small remaining pile below. That first descent was the most scary. Looking down, the distance always seemed much greater than looking up.

Like forbidden fruit, these mountains were there and eventually we no longer resisted their temptation. Climbing up and sliding down the pile was an activity banned by Dad. His concern was not so much for our safety; rather, he did not want the hay messed up. Little harm came to the tall pile but the landing pad was soon scattered, making it that much more difficult to pitch the hay from.

Once on top of the stack, our reasoning was that one or two slides would not hurt anything. One or two slides did not really show but the cumulative effect of the dozens of slides, long after everyone forgot about counting, certainly did. The enjoyment of sliding and landing in the soft hay soon gave way to concern for possible consequences. Not only was the hay scattered, but, it also was threshed and broken. If we pitched the hay back on to the pile we thought Dad would not notice.

These piles of hay were the main food supply for the cattle until the spring grass emerged from the thawed earth. Sometimes, there just was not enough hay and the farmers were forced to buy some elsewhere or rely on any remaining pile of straw for the meagre food value it provided.

I recall one winter which was particularly harsh and long. Before the snow melted, we ran out of both hay and straw. What a feeling of helplessness — the hungry cattle were weak, cows were giving birth and needed extra food to supply enough milk for the calves, and there was no feed for them. Our situation was not unique, as other farmers were faced with the same problem. Eventually, we resorted to hauling sleigh loads of straw from a field two miles away. Luckily, this pile, although two years old, was of good quality straw and was not needed by the farmer. Others less fortunate came and hauled it away one load at a time. Keeping the cattle filled up with this straw meant a daily trip to this quickly diminishing pile.

Don't shun your own.

With the completion of harvest, it seemed that the evenings quickly ate away at the short daylight hours, until, we found ourselves in the house long before it was time to go to bed. Initially, our home was lit with a small, glass-covered coal oil lamp. If the wick was not trimmed properly, the glass constantly needed cleaning. Later, as the evenings became longer, we used a two-mantle lamp which was hung from the ceiling and gave off a very bright light. Since this lamp was more delicate and difficult to light, Dad was the sole operator.

The magic of the light switch, instantly flooding a room with light, was not part of our farm life until 1956, when I was thirteen years old. Most of the farmers in our area finally agreed to pay for the installation of miles of electrical wires strung from tall poles. Electricity on the farm was undoubtedly the single most important event which changed our life in so many ways.

Before its wide use, evenings were indeed very long, and the houses, whether by the dim light of wick lamps or by the bright light of two-mantle lamps, were filled with a variety of activities, most of which were centred around the kitchen table. The kitchen was the most important room in the house and was the only room with a light in it. Card games were very popular among both adults and children. For an hour or so each evening, we also listened to the battery-operated radio. The thick frost on the kitchen window provided a surface where we spent a great deal of time making coin impressions in the ice. Your goal was to create a perfect impression of the coins and this activity ended when you ran out of useable ice surface.

Winter evenings were also a time for lessons conducted by one of the parents. The main purpose of these lessons was to learn to read and write Ukrainian. Until the thirty-two letter Cyrillic alphabet, very different from the alphabet learned at school, was mastered, these readings sessions were quite painful. However, we were constantly told by our parents that, one day, we would thank them for taking time to teach us. This has indeed been very true, in my case, as the ability to read and write Ukrainian has opened up another world.

As we became more fluent in reading, we were introduced to various aspects of our ethnic background. Most importantly, I was introduced to the work of Taras Shevchenko, a poet of Ukraine. In one of his poems, he urges his people to gain knowledge, to think and to learn from others, but, in the process, not to allow this newfound knowledge to become so important that you forget who your mother is. Learn from others, but, do not shun your own is a phrase with as much meaning today as when it was first written well over one hundred years ago.

The carollers are coming.

Christmas, because of the festivities, food, gifts and visiting, was an exciting time of the year. For our family, the day before Christmas, especially the evening which began with the sighting of the first star, was the most important.

Mom spent all day preparing a minimum of twelve meatless dishes, most essential of which was kutia, a mixture of boiled wheat, poppy seeds and honey. After all the animals were fed, Dad brought in some hay and a sheaf of wheat called a didukh. Some of the hay was arranged in a thin layer on the table, before Mom covered it with an embroidered linen tablecloth, and the rest was placed under the table. The didukh was set in a corner of the kitchen.

While the older children helped Mom set the table, the younger ones were kept busy running to the window to look out for the first star.

This was a holy supper, during which little conversation took place. It was an emotional time, when all present remembered those who were no longer alive. The extra chair and place setting at the table was a link with the past, as it was believed that the souls of the dead were present during the meal.

When all preparations were complete, the family, dressed in their finest clothes, began the meal with a prayer. This was followed by kutia, which Dad served in small quantities to all family members, with wishes for good luck and happiness in the coming year. The other dishes were then served, and everyone was expected to sample each one. The slow pace of the meal was difficult for us as we were excited and could hardly wait to finish and go under the table to play in the hay.

There, in the hay, to bring good luck to the family in the New Year, we made various animal sounds as we looked for nuts, candy, and other treats our parents had hidden. Any gifts were distributed sometime during the evening and before going to bed we all sang carols.

Christmas Day was spent going to church and later, after evening chores were done, visiting with one of the neighbouring families. In their farmhouse, filled with the aroma of large quantities of food and the smell of cigarette smoke, we snatched a candy or orange here, a nut or two there, while we walked or ran back and forth between the kitchen and the other large room of the house. After more people arrived our traffic lanes were blocked by sitting or standing bodies and we had to crawl under tables, chairs and benches to get to where the most interesting conversation or card game was taking place. With time, the men became very involved in their game of King Pedro, occasionally interrupting it with loud arguments.

During the evening, a group of carollers, carrying a star, arrived. The host and hostess, after making a monetary contribution, offered them something to eat and drink before they ventured out in the cold to the next farmhouse. Carollers, usually young men and women representing the neighbouring country churches, made their rounds during the three days of Christmas and we looked forward to their visitations. Some years, due to the severe cold and snow-blocked roads Christmas activities were limited, as the only means of transportation was by horse and sleigh.

It's your turn to come over on Sunday.

Since we lived a half mile from the country school, there was no real need for us, as children, to have our own horse and sleigh for transportation purposes. This, in some ways, was a distinct disadvantage, especially when it came to visiting at night. We had no choice but to rely on other children, who lived further from school, and had their own transportation, or, we walked. Quite often, we walked the mile or two to our neighbours and spent a winter evening visiting. On a cold night, these distances were great, especially to anyone with short legs.

Today, when I go back to the farm and retrace the roads we walked, it seems that the distances have shrunk. Such is the case with many aspects of my childhood world, as distance and size of objects have all become smaller.

Our visits usually consisted of staying indoors and playing a variety of card games, or Monopoly, a new game which became increasingly popular. We, also, just sat and told stories. It was during visiting sessions, such as these, that the deeds of last Hallowe'en were retold, and, without fail, the conversation led to talk of ghosts and stories about the dead. Since the older people were often superstitious, their own tales added fuel to what we discussed. Although these were popular topics, they were not really appreciated by those who still had to walk home in the dark.

Invariably, someone tried to ease the conversation about ghosts, by retelling the story of a mouse, who for weeks frightened the occupants of a house by walking around in the attic, dragging a mousetrap, attached to its tail. This story was an example of how most ghost stories had a simple explanation.

Before leaving for home, we were always treated to a lunch of sandwiches, coffee and sweets. Then, it was time to get bundled up and begin the trip home. We did not look forward to leaving the warm, cosy atmosphere of the neighbour's farmhouse. Somehow, the distance home always seemed so much farther.

On a cold, crisp, clear night sounds carried very far. As you walked, the squeaking of the snow under your boots seemed so loud. Occasionally, when you stopped to listen, the silence was disturbed by distant sounds of a dog barking or a coyote howling. Beyond these sounds the bright winter night was very stark, cold and quiet. A distant, faint light of a farmhouse was your only sign of life.

To help make the walk home not seem so long, it was common practice to have someone walk partway home with you. Your visit officially ended when you parted company and everyone hurried home along the moonlit road.

I saw something moving . . .

Small country churches, each with its own cemetary, were scattered across the farming communities of the prairies. Two such churches were located just across the road from our farmyard.

The proximity of the churches did not bother us, but the cemetaries did, especially after a burial of someone from the community. Going outside, alone in the dark, was not something any of us volunteered to do. This fear of the dead gradually diminished as we grew older, but, periodically, it was rekindled by another death or a ghost storytelling session. Most of this fear was brought on by vivid imaginations, as well as by parents who added fuel with their own superstitions and stories.

I was greatly affected emotionally by the untimely death of my grandfather. For a seven year old child, all the grieving and the return of the body to the family home, where it remained during the night, and the long church service, followed by the burial, was a very powerful series of events.

Fear of ghosts, death and cemetaries affected the Shostak children but not nearly as much as it did the others in the farm community. For several youngsters, going past the cemetary at night was a highly nerve-racking experience. During the many ghost story episodes, we related our ordeals of travelling past the cemetaries. Each of us had his or her own method. Some felt that the best way was to walk quickly without looking back, until you were well past the grave markers when it was safe to run; others either whistled or sang, hoping not to think about their surroundings; while others literally went around the problem area by taking a wide detour through the fields. This latter solution was not possible during most of the year. The number of night visitors we received was definitely affected by our dead neighbours across the road.

One late fall evening, two neighbouring sixteen year old boys, on horseback, came over to our home where they sat talking with my father well into the night. All the while, they seemed a bit uneasy, and my father wondered what they were up to as they took turns going outside.

Several days later, we learned that the purpose of their frequent trips outdoors was to listen for the sound of their peers returning home from an evening of visiting. The two lads, after quickly departing from our home, went to one of the cemetaries, where, dressed in white sheets, they hid behind the grave markers and awaited the returning visitors.

Later, many versions, each more flowery and elaborate, were retold of this event.

Everyone is finally asleep.

The one room which we could call our own was located in the upstairs attic area of the house. Not only did it serve as our sleeping quarters, but it also was our playroom. Winter-time play was limited since we did not have our own light source. Most of our light was provided by the one window located at the south end of the room. A small amount of light also came up the stairwell from the kitchen. Seated on the two beds, in the dimly lit room, we spent many evenings exchanging stories and playing games which did not require much light.

Here in the privacy of our rooms, we avidly read and reread our comic books. Recent acquisitions could be found under the mattress of our bed. Although this reading material was not altogether banned by our parents, any purchase of new comics was frowned upon. However, when we did go to town, we could not resist buying at least one new edition from our twenty-five cent allowance. You could purchase a regular comic book for a dime, or, on occasion, it was possible to buy a special fifty-two pager. Once the purchase was made, it was hidden and secretly removed to the seclusion of our room. Trading at school, a daily occurrence, was also carried out without the knowledge of our parents or teachers. Each morning I left for school with several books hidden in my felt boots or tucked under my shirt.

Although the bright winter moon illumin-ated our room, before falling asleep we took care to close the curtains so that this light would not shine on us as we slept. It was our belief that moonlight on your head was the cause of nightmares.

Heat, radiating from the chimney and metal pipe, as well as warm air from the kitchen, kept the room quite comfortable, except during the very severe winter coldspells. On these occasions, you did not fool around getting ready for bed. After quickly undressing down to your longjohns, you crawled under the thick covers and remained curled in a ball, until the warmth of your body made it possible to uncover your face. As the bed warmed, you slowly uncurled, and your legs slid further down the mattress, pushing the cold out.

The luxury of sleeping alone was unheard of, and as a result, we had to contend with a variety of irritations and inconveniences caused by our sleeping partner. There was nothing more uncomfortable than sleeping on a bed with weak springs with a much heavier person. The weight of the heavy person sloped the bed to the centre and your only solution was to sleep hanging onto the side. Other irritations included a companion who hogged the covers or was suffering from a bad cold and accompanying cough.

In the wintertime, you were in bed early, usually long before you were tired. There was time for plenty of fooling around before every-one fell asleep. These nights could sure be long.

We acknowledge the following
collectors whose work appears in this
publication:

 Artists' Reproductions of Thought
 Alexander D. Gontar
 Roman and Theresa Herchak
 Hollander York Gallery
 Mr. and Mrs. Bob Hope
 Bruce and Dolly Lansdowne
 Christine Maruschak
 Dr. and Mrs. M. Myckatyn
 Paperworks Gallery
 Dr. and Mrs. J. Shudrak
 Stephen and Maria Shumelda
 Mr. and Mrs. Ross Shwaikoski
 Tippet - Richardson Limited
 Dr. and Mrs. Robert Wallace
 Dr. Lorraine Wright